ANGELA GREENE

SILENCE AND THE BLUE NIGHT

SALMON POETRY

First published in 1993 by
Salmon Publishing Limited,
A division of Poolbeg Enterprises Ltd,
Knocksedan House,
Swords, Co. Dublin, Ireland.

A catalogue record for this book is available from the British Library.

ISBN 1 897648 06 5

Photograph by Mike O'Toole
Cover design by Poolbeg Group Services Ltd
Set by Mac Book Limited in Palatino
Printed by The Guernsey Press Limited,
Vale, Guernsey, Channel Islands

Potato

*Inside of one potato
there are mountains and rivers.*

Shinkichi Takahashi
Translated by Harold P. Wright

Acknowledgements are due to the editors of the following
where some of these poems appeared for the first time:

*Trio Poetry 6 (Blackstaff Press); New Women Poets (Bloodaxe
Books); Slants of Light (C.J. Fallon); Poets Aloud;
Writing Women (UK); The Irish Press; Poetry Ireland Review;
Outposts (UK); Envoi (UK); The Honest Ulsterman;
Barbican 1 & 2; Verse (UK); The Sunday Tribune; Poetry Wales;
Other Poetry (UK); The Rialto (UK); Footnotes -S.P.A. (UK).*

Some of the work published in this collection has also been
read on *RTE Radio* and *BBC Radio Ulster* and has been per-
formed in *Sunny Side Plucked* at the Project Arts Centre, Dublin.

*The author wishes to acknowledge the sponsorship of
Patrick Carroll & Company in the Patrick Kavanagh Award.*

This book is for Austin

CONTENTS

I

II

III

I

DESTINY

Then her eyelids were the damson's bloom
and her cheeks were ripe.
Then her hair flossed umber shadows
down the sweep of her creamy nape,
and the tips of her lively hands shone
like peeled almonds.

Her blue dress and her snowy apron were crisp
and she sang as she worked,
deftly patient with those in her charge.

Then she got married, and in that free
and giddy twenties way
she sat astride their first motorbike.

Where apple blossom pollened the lanes
they tumbled their burning kisses
into waves of cool grass.

Then pregnant, again and again
her breasts
were the moist cambric of the midnight hours.

She rose early. To bake bread
and to launder by oil light;
or pulling the blinds for the sun's warm splash,
she worked
till those folded nights blotted her damp skin.

I was happy one day close in her milky scent
when he came home early;
my father, and the midwife in her navy coat,
and those soft eyes nudged me outdoors.

Through the clear glass, when I stood on tiptoe,
I saw her thighs
heaped like bruised poppies onto the white sheet.

I shush by that April window
till, in its searchings, her voice finds me out.
Its thin cries pierce me.
They sift down my blood like blown seed
from somewhere
                          far off.

ENCOUNTER

In a garden planted
round a lake, she knew
a secret tree, would go there
often; a high hostess to
crows, and ferns knitted over
harled and varicosed roots.

Above a bank, thronged
with tiny things, swung
one low branch to idle on.
There she lay, one neutral
Sunday, satisfied, in a
new daisy-patterned frock;

ears alive to black
mammies scolding overhead,
the moored protest of
the old boat on the lake;
she craved attention. When
progress of people, trespassing

by her tree, fuelled
her childishness, she
jumped down, called her
name then, twirled and
twirled and twirled so
wild she made daisies

flare, and curtsied before
the wrapped-around rug
of a man seated in a
wheeled chair. With bright
coffee bean eyes he smiled.
I like your frock, and

I like your name, child.
My name is Douglas Hyde.
Go, dance your fairy dance.
Dance child dance.
She held her secret
like a daisy holds light.

TURNING POINT

Tap dance lesson shows me time is motion:
it is never to stay still.
My new red shoes, like seed beans jumping
inside their bag, hungry for
the music of my feet,
I am first in Miss O'Hara's big bare room
to raise the piano lid, set records out.

When the older girls burst in, smug
behind lips tinted plum or coral,
we younger ones must practice,
'In the corner, please, last week's
shuffle-ball-flat-twirl-and-twirl.'

However hard I try,
I can't forget the school knickers I still wear,
long, navy-blue and thick.

And now the big girls,
in scant blue skirts and tops, are lining up
all set to attempt that new routine
they've seen perfected by the Royalettes,
and the keyboard warms
to Miss O'Hara's long red fingertips.

Slowly, it starts, then, I watch
their united skill and confidence let feet
automatically
tap out that rhythm mine still balk at.

Arms rest lightly on each other's hips,
heads bold above chiffon throats, breasts pointed;
then, right, front, lift, swing left, legs kick
thigh high for adolescent heats'
swirl to incense the air.

Transfixed, out of tune and slumped
in the corner, I am staring
at the flushed efforts of these intent
and future chorus girls:
I see their white thin briefs stained pink,
their stretched blue armpits sweated through.

WASTELAND

You gave us the solid stuff of living:
early rising, well brushed teeth
and hair, kitchen skills, needlework,
the rhythm of sown seed; facts
kept warm in a brown hen's clutch
and, at each day's start and finish, prayer.

We knew that Sunday silk and a tilted straw
was not a fancy to mask
the ordinary life, or soften
the conviction in your deeper self,
but a ploy of symmetry
you used in your need to remain afloat.

I watched you, wretched in double tragedy,
stay upright on your rock of hope
though wave after mountainous wave
of sorrow should have unmade you.
When that force engulfed me it was your
strength supported my sinking spirit.

Staunch mother
who had to re-learn long days unaided
but for safe activity and prayer;
I admire your courage. Now my life
seems empty of all those things I knew
I invoke deft hand, resolute mind
to come as lodestar to this narrowed waste.

MOTHER

If there were times our sameness seemed a trial,
our jealousies and piques frothed layer on layer,

rest in peace. You win. For even in death
your body chose a dignity and beauty all its own.

Friends startle now at my very likeness to you;
your body language, your tone of voice.

As if I'd presumed to imitate you.
You and I know the difference. And I

can still enter that bedroom afternoon
with your filmy eyes grown girlish to see

in its red, yellow-ribboned box,
the honey and almond layer cake I bring you

hot from the Teatime Express –
a small brightness for your deep loneliness

we scoop and enjoy in mute content.
For you are tired with years. Your head slips

back into your new childish sleep. I watch how
minus the weight of worlds your features

resume their original grace; how the late
winter sun excites the silver of your hair.

I touch your skin, the awe in its cambric fineness,
then, let gently fall the bedclothes over your hands

laid in feathery-relief on your bird-like breast.
I tidy tea things, glad to gather and store the gift

of this moment when it is clear, mother,
that we touch only what we both know has no words.

A LIFE

Were you the swelled bodice moist with milk;
bowlsful of brown eggs on a yellow tabletop,
buttermilk bread, the jacket on floury potatoes?

Were you the icing on a cake melted
into one summer birthday;
the magician of the treadle,
a drawer full of useless things?

Were you the dark mornings of the Nine Fridays,
the flowered straw at the evening meet;
the hard grey eyes of temper,
the hands of silk on well-soaped limbs?

Were you the cold holy water thrown after poltergeist,
the hot, china teapot flung in a rage;
the fierce pride of a slammed door,
the open hand to the hungry child?

Were you the tissue paper on flapper's finery,
the outraged at Hollywood's latest;
the lamp's-glow mothing children,
the ceaseless care of the aged?

Were you the art of living
clinched in that brittle diminishing round...

You are a sprig of rosemary at a wake.
You are a handful of clay on a coffin lid.

THE PATH

That time you brought me
by a curved path
over two fields to school.
My small hand cautious
in your palm, we walked,
silent and strained,
where the mayflower
formed a roadside hedge,
heavy and still,
to shield us from the world.

And I remember
how good it felt
having you all to myself,
and the way the cinder path
squeaked beneath our hurried feet.
You left me at the school gate.

And though the bell for class
had long gone I stood
watching you go back
by that same path –
a child, her senses
clogged with tears, who wanted
to be your special one
if the awkwardness
that broke the father-daughter
love-circuit had allowed.

ULSTER ELEMENT

That time the telegram arrived,
you dumb at its words, confounding me
with a grandmother's existence and death –
'Are we, or not, to attend her funeral?'

And I search your face, wanting to find
a tear, a quiver, anything to open
these floodgates to your past
where I might float secure on my own story.
But your body is chiselled stone.
I circle, closely, Mother's tears and prayers,
aware of stirrings out-fathoming her grief.

A second telegram states: 'Immediate
interment stop remains oedematous stop.'

They bury her without us near Strabane:
and I am the child who strains both ear and mind
to weave into the thin tapestry of my life
this Presbyterian woman stiff with pride
who'd spent her lifetime swallowing bitter tears,
to bulk it now with this waterlogged grandmother.

I grasp, in fear, the edge of this dark fact
and sense such order must be the will of things.
Her money changes nothing. Makes no waves,
turns no tides. The severing silence of years
still defines its border round our lives.

Christmas, years later, your head bent sipping port,
you seem unable to dam the blinding sadness
spilling into your glass and you turn,
in a harsh aside to me,
'She was as hard as nails you know,'
and deftly you down your tear-charged drink.

THE LOST GARDEN

In here time waits.
Bees trade in the pollened air,
drugging the scented levels.
Fruit trees, roses and border pinks
lose their grip to a smother
of brambles and scutch –
a springy undergrowth made slithery
with cankered branch bits
and ginger leaves.

Red admirals are balletic,
embroidering nettle clumps
to marigolds. Along the hedge,
the white-faced elderflowers
flare in a dazzle of light,
and a thrush springs
to crack the seal on a snail's brown box.

The fountain eats moss, its source
a boss of leathery docks. Here
and there, lavender
and pale green leaves bush,
their buds stuck with cuckoo-spit.
The everywhere vetch and bindweed
puzzle and twist.

Days close on cauls of webs,
cadenzas of twitterings, then
cat's eyes, sudden among inky shadows.
Where hart's-tongue whiskers the cob-wall
and the ivy reaches thicken,
the glasshouse frame sinks
to its bed of smashed glass.

And out there, beyond that wall,
in the high-rise, the plastic world,
the great earth-eaters rear
with monstrous jaws, poised
to consume, consume.

No Man's Land

White lace frets her blue
wrapped silence as she walks
in no man's land from a dream
of death under a heart fluttering
truce to moon and grave, large eyes
scavenging joy at a glass door.

She uses tactics of an idle
woman in her unequal war.
Bathing and silking her slackened
body out of its distorted memory.
Blushing blood of exotic labels onto
her pale cheeks, painting her nails

like any pretty woman, flossing
her hair about her face. A
primeval will of flesh demanding
discipline. Out there, they are awed
by the fragrance of her shawled privacy.
Envious of her flower-filled room.

An administrative army, suckling
and napping at ease on
rumpled beds. How could they know
in her branded room, 'no visitors'
or cards shook their congratulations.
That she lay often, mute,

encrusted in despair. That,
at night, at a cold window as
her name called in passing
she resisted and darkness swept
innocence away. While, out there,
they suckled their joy and

chattered away unaware
of the viable beat a radio pulsed
around them, as it was
switched on, casually.

CHRISTENING ROBE

The bundle, like a soft toy,
slipped from the top shelf,
concealed in haste

the day before I left the hospital.
Unfolding its expectant newness,
I imagine your head cusped

in dark down above this
loosed froth of lace,
your face pink and puckering

as the priest pours your name
over you. Startled, your hands
windmill a breath away

from my heart. My mind
swells as I fumble with slippery
ribbons, lay handfuls of lace

over putto feet. When I gather
you close, from somewhere deep
comes a low, long cry.

RED BUTTERFLIES

If, for you I had prepared a scented garden,
not this draggled patch stitched with brier

but a sanctuary, of honey-coloured stonework
where I had Albertine roses hung.

If I had sown a lawn of pennyroyal
would the air have been a balm about your play

and, if I had thought to plant the snow-ball bush
would your small hand have stroked its
                                  earth-bound task.

If I had slung a cushioned hammock between
two lilac trees, would you have leaned there

drifting on the blossom of a dream, and,
had I but known to net the wingbreath

of two red butterflies

would they have been your lungs on days when
                                  breathing hurt,
or carried you beyond the crush of pain.

ELEGY

November, and my dead
crowd me. New-born,
you died before I saw you.

O, these years without you.
Yet you are always with me –
the words of a sad song
I can not complete.

Your infant limbs curl
in these syllables. You sleep
safe in sheets of soft white.

In other women's babies I look
for you. I pick among shells
for one fragment of you.

                    In the grass,
or high in the buds of Spring
where I almost hear you,
the wind shifts,
and its cry opens in blue air.

In the places children gather
I search and find, again and again,
that strange emptiness.

Asleep I see you, whole-limbed,
tall, running in the wind –
but awake the dream has kept you . . .

And you are where I must learn
to leave you, safe
with the dead. November,
old memories fret,
and my dead crowd me.

Garden Epitaphs

You were my elder brother
brave rowan tree
ousting winter with a sun-white flare.
Your leaves and berries
                                        bleed
the autumn mists.

You were my younger brother
purple clematis
                                        struggling
in ivy; wind-torn, rain-washed, still
your eager-faced blooms thrust.

You were my infant son
flowering malus;
all of your angel-skinned buds
                                        blossom
to a perfect nimbus in blue-blue air.

You were my mother
                                winter cherry
the 60-watt glow in grey weather.
A grief of opal tints
disturbs your summer green.

You my father, the contorted oak,
stand where your old friend the sun
                        attends you
yet light is a hurt among your awkward leaves.
What aches in your coiling trunk
that you refuse
to fling wide your locked arms.

II

ON THE EDGE

But what if, instead of cooking dinner to-night I
       flew out to New York.
What wild words are these? Where do they come from?
What urges the hand that shapes them?
They are not mine: no more than the water
gushing from this tap rinsing these vegetables,
or the downpour raining its long sorrow
       on the windscreen of New York.
But what if to-night I flew out to New York.

Here's a woman in cardboard city. She holds
a raw potato in her hand.
       She's not cooking dinner. She's planting
tubers in her Palisades backyard
                          a Hudson of skies ago.
And not even such dark rain could start her weeping.

This night that wet smoke and the screaming sirens
       have made jumpy,
stumbles and falls on the scorched and beaten
body down on One Hundred and Forty-First shifting
the stink of guilt from nameless back to
nameless back. But what if I try
to think this violence and these sounds unreal...

Here I am standing in the rain on Fifth Avenue.
Where cabs, like yellow dinosaurs, stampede, crammed
with sharp and glittering faces lusting
       for the coupledom of dinner.

Thin as a candle, I peer up into the blackness
this city jabs lit and flashing,
       like knives, like daggers...
And somehow or other all of the creatures
              in their time-ridden rooms bring sobs
and claws inside my skull.   Then scatter each ripped
nerve onto the wind
                            turning the sky to splinters.
I am rags of grief.

I walk up to the blind black man.
The one whose hair is made of light.
He is offering his begging box. I lean
far into his eyeballs
                     and would drown
in those twin rivers of agony and shadow.
But I adjust the seasoning of his dinner
and change my whole style of giving.

A fog of heat comes up from underneath. It licks,
rising like fear about my feet. Like the steam
       that boils off cauldrons...
I breathe in the deathly flavour, and all the time
       a bright river of blood -
the rage of all the crushed ones,
shrieks its message
                     DON'T WALK. DON'T WALK.

For a long time I have lived
with a pearl in my mouth
                     inside the knife
that threatens to prise my shell wide open.

Now my dream has gone off somewhere. Pained
by the waste of skies and bridges caught
         inside this Apple.
By these eyes that the glass and the concrete
         have made sleepless. Jittery.
Living on the edge.

BOMB

....and then, above the night-quiet trees,
the grass curled up in soft hollows,
across the contented acres
of the Phoenix Park a star
falls to the ground crying.
A thud. An instant when the whole world turns
on and off its lights. Then, nothing
but the night shivering at the windowpane.

At dawn, crater and rubble were there,
nothing else by the grove
where the warden and his small daughter lived.
I leaned over. Where she would sleep
now, that little girl, verged on obsession...

I mull on it still –
When cries fall in the night.
When the grass and the trees
outstare me with their greenness,
and earth lies sleeping
under a sky loaded with stars.

TERRORIST'S WIFE

A phone-call takes him
into the dark for weeks.
In the mornings, his absence
fills me with dread. I thin my eyes
to watch for cars that come to wait
down in the street. All day
I move from room to room. I polish
each spotless place
to a chill shining. Fear tracks me
like hunger. In the silence,
the walls grow wafer-thin.
The neighbours wear masks –
tight lips, veiled looks, such
fine tissues of knowing.
My mother doesn't visit. I drag
my shopping from the next town.

Once, putting his clean shirts away,
my dry hands touched a shape
that lay cold and hard. I wept then,
and walked for hours in the park.
I listened for his name in the news.
When I looked at our sleeping son
my sadness thickened.
His comings are like his goings –
a swift movement in the night.

At times, he can sit here for days
meticulously groomed; primed,
watching soccer games on TV,
our child playful on his lap.

But scratch the smooth surface
of his mood, and how
the breached defences spit their fire.

Now, when he holds me to him,
I know I taste murder
on his mouth. And in the darkness,
when he turns from me, I watch him
light a cigarette. In his palm
the lighter clicks and flames.
Balanced, incendiary.

ENNISKILLEN

This town is always morning
inside my skull: with slant light
on the slant roofs; the people
coiling into the streets. And
something always just about
to happen. I am caught forever
in the cold ache of it.

I see a long, black car
enter the town with flowers
on its roof glinting like frost.
As if from far away it comes,
out of the morning light, edging
through the hushed crowd to
the war memorial where it stands,
throbbing in the silent air. Then
slowly, purposefully, in the grey light,
it moves on towards our church.

As in a dream I gaze
till my eyes grow dim from watching it.
Then suddenly, into the zone
of hearing comes a fierce cracking sound,
and the pain in a young girl's scream.
And all about is noise
and confusion and everywhere
is stained with poppies.

Motionless, I feel
a weight like stone crush my heart,

and hear a voice that is sure
with love. Each time I make
to raise my body to investigate
a soft, warm hand clutches mine...

CÉZANNE

Scatters pears and apples
onto the rumpled tablecloth
to tantalise; he leaves
the boy in the red vest
propped on his elbow to ponder
that right arm's long reach.
He has in mind landscapes
where trees, rocks and skies
become the spaces
he renders solid with colour.
Massed jewels
would be this vibrant.
He lets his joy flicker
in the pinks, creams and lilacs on a jug,
and tightens the edges of the world
with light. His worst dream
is of a portrait sitter whose features
shift. He struggles with his lust
for a mountain,
purpled and blue-white as a breast,
which he cannot resist.

VISITOR – COLDEN VALLEY

- at Arvon Foundation, Lumb Bank

Stepped into what seemed a May-soft, water-lit place
that, reaching out, included me in its parade
of beech-green and birch-silver along innocent,
wet banks above the skitter of the bright beck's
downrush. So safe.

Drawn by the hill's craggy face
in sunlight, the millstack elegant in high
jet beading; not until I'd crossed the bridge
and stood, did they explode their fire inside my skull.
The words: the smoulderings of legend
the women gave out.

Of this millyard's looms
which wove nothing but black silk to clothe
the cleft hearts of the widows; how work-raw children,
on this track, went into the wind their cries had become.
How stone and ground were shut over crushed
and stunted lives.

Suddenly I am caught in it:
the brute misery rooted in this valley; compelled
to touch, to risk the burden of the stone's
brooding silence: part of how the world knows
its grief and pain filtering through us, is what
cries in the dark, disturbs dreams.

RECIPE

(The following recipe was copied word for word out of an old manuscript recipe book. The exact date is not known, but one item in the book is dated 1790.)

THE DUMFRIESSHIRE COOKERY BOOK, 1935

Drop Biscuits: The far, far famed Lincolnshire Drop.

7 eggs (the middle-sized are proper), well beat up,
18 oz of double refined sugar sifted twice,
15 oz of flour dried the day before.
The ingredients must be quite cold.

The quicker in making drop biscuits
the better and lighter they will be – drop them
upon dried cap paper (not warm), with a spoon,
just round them as quickly as you can in the middle.

To glaze them have ready a little double
refined sugar to dredge over them through gauze.
Slip them off the paper with a large bread knife
the instant they come from the oven or the paper
will not come off at all if this is not attended to.

None in England to equal these for beauty
and excellence. It is a little fortune
to gain into this grand secret,
and have been at it for many years to obtain it. Only
just gently stir in the flour; bake 8 mins.

VAN GOGH'S ROOM IN ARLES

Night room we see by day:
where shadow is suppressed
and colour
does everything to penetrate
our defence against reality.

This is his way of creating
a calm, of reaching
into peace, of making a place
other to escape the violent world
he suffers.

And these flat washes furnish –

A few portraits on pale violet walls,
red floor-tiles, green window, lilac
doors; a blue jug upon an orange table.
The broad, fresh-buttery yellow
line of bed and chair, and everywhere
the light
             striking
clean colours that soothe.

This is his new dreamed-of room:
with each coherent space the imagination's
nirvana.
             In this room nothing
is shuttered.

We watch this unique harmony of simple things.
Our minds at rest.
                        We wait.
And when he comes
                        dizzy
from the suction of the turnsole sun,
the black despair of cypresses, mute writhings
that are olive trees, that fireball rush
of stars,
            to throw

his shuddering, misfit body
onto the lemon-green cool sheets, we know
his burning head will flame,
                                become again
that fierce, first blaze,
                        the first
rotating sunflower.

SHELL TALK

Sea shells are filled
with stories to interest
any human ear that wants to know.
Wet-bright, we come
chattering from the ocean's wash
to spread our gossip
on this dull beach.

Listen at our frilly lips!
We see dark waters ebb
and flow against deserted shores
where girls with polished limbs
once moved in dance. We know
of treasure, sunk
and dimmed, in unfamiliar

watery depths, and press pink
curves into the cavities of
the drowned who lie staring
from sad tenements of wrecks
hoping for the sun. Where fronds
slow-finger coral reefs
we linger, then journey, grieving,
on the dying echo of the blue whale's cry.

Sometimes, tuned to an ancient memory,
we call to each other down
the windslopes with sounds like the sea.
But mostly, voices harsh from trading
talk of land-locked things, and boots,
with heavy tread, come
carelessing our lives, and our lore,
unheeded, is shattered underfoot.

TIDE-MARKS

Tide-marks in sand. Years
etched by water. Tide
going back...makes
simple domestic shapes. Kitchen-
sieve mesh slackening
to garden trellis beside
this froth of petticoat tails.

           Tide

going back...works an intricate
design fit for a royal wrist, if
sand were lace. Here
is the linen-fold found in the great halls.
Here the harp, swelled
with its ancient music...

           Follow

this spider's web of trade routes,
that march of Greek-key to these
crumbling bits – the scattered
treasuries, and ruins
abandoned in haste.

           These peaks

are the cold, inner heights
of the Alps, and elephants' ears
stiff in the wind. And, over there
the gentle forest hushed now
after the battle... Sand, parched,
beyond this stringy grass is home
to nomad bands, their wide-eyed babies.

                              And tracks,
tracks always made my feet
and hooves trekking slowly down
to cross the scorched plains... And
in the distance, the heat-haze shimmering
on the wide expanse of sand
with the sun sizzling
the backs of men who drag stones in Egypt...

SILENCE AND THE BLUE NIGHT

Here is the place
you would want to arrive at
after a long journey preceded
by grief and much delay.
There is a brown mountain.
Lavender clouds roof a sea
so wide and level the image
blanks the mind. Night is falling.
From the terrace you see a farmhouse
with ochred arches lit
from within. Its beasts are settled,
folded into rest. It is a scene
of domestic tenderness
offering its warmth.

                    But
it is too artful a backdrop
for the mother
calling anxiously to her child.
He has wandered off
beyond the rocks to the sea
leaving his blue bag spilling
its contents over the red tiles.
She calls his pet name, twice,
but the third call becomes
a frail and exotic sound –
some primitive bird's perhaps?

She risks the rough ground, mind
racing, she is
already elsewhere her torchlight
a flame plunging through lakes
of blue air. Now the clouds are
deeper purple, agitating darkly
to loose and grab at the moon.
In hot dust, among dry stones,
she stumbles; lizards
crackle in the scrub. The rocks
are full of shadows. The sea is a
hiss on distant shingle.

Again she calls but her cry
falls in thin and difficult
echoes and is absorbed
into the mountain. Is the name
really a name, or a memory
unravelling inside her skull?
Is she calling her child
or is she
the child being called?
She has forgotten where she is.

                         She stands.
Night deepens, merciless.
The lit farmhouse, the terrace
with its globe of light
are out of reach now. Like ships
becalmed on a sea of dark,

they are remote, inhuman. She dips
the torchbeam. Around her
the indigo stillness glooms.
Silence and the blue night
engulf the boy
whose pale limbs she is desperate
to arrange in sleep.

THE UPPER ROOM

Have you
ever baked a crisp brown loaf
a batch of crunchy scones
chocolate cake dark and rich and
have you
just before the oven closed
crossed your work and begged
heaven raise the dough, and
have you
cooled and set the feast before
a brood gone wild with hunger, and
have you
sat dreaming, sipping tea
sensed the presence of
an unobtrusive guest who
seems quite at home,
breaking bread in the heart of your
family.

AUBADE FOR A SCHOOLBOY
for Richard

To come into your room
to find your dark head
sloped back on blue pillows
soft-snoring, your glasses
firm on your nose, automobile
catalogues, with fantastic

calculations and notes
in the margin, dropped
near you, strange music
drifting to the ceiling,
I know you are cruising
under the fixed stars

in your red mini-car
over remote desert sands,
or heedless of time,
tinkering in the greased
mysteries under a sleek
vintage-type bonnet:

how can I wake you
to the drabness of this
boxed-in life before
you glimpse one streak
of slivery dawn or
know the thrust and speed
of your own power?

CHAIN

for Miriam

I cradle you at dawn.
You suck noisily
warm milk, in this hour I savour
before birds fuss to disturb
mother and daughter, now
signed and sworn.
I have reached a promised land
with you, gift child
milk and honey of another

love born; let a brighter hour
make that clear: to receive
in joy we must give in pain.
And, now, daughter in my
sunlit season I must make hay;
watch you pick daisies for a chain
to link us three,
forever
I will think of her,
as she,
I do not doubt,
will think of me.

STIRRING
for Ruth

Pots are muttering on the lowest heat
in the kitchen. Stony-faced, on the mat
in front of the stove, she sits, in pigtails,
torn blue jeans, stained runners, clutching
a fat black cat. Her pale cheek is pressed
on his furred cheek; his sleek paw
is curved to her rigid shoulder; his
purr is stilled sensing this fierce,
first struggle. I work around them.

It was here she built her leaning towers,
acted princess to the legendary frog;
would soar weightless, drifting for hours
within her very own wonderland.
She used to throw her anguish onto my neck,
drained each scalding hurt into my ear.
For this brittle world she is entering she chooses
an animal's embrace, a stove's warmth

and what magic adheres to an old mat.

MONDAY'S MOTHER

She drags it like a hod of coals, each
Monday; heaves the black, rough load
of her mood. Brood released, bearing, trucelike,
foul clothes across sour-smelling rooms. Push
open the grime of the windows to free
squarely the week-end's war cries, its energetic
music. It stifles her, Monday's lumpy spill,
the house filthy and sullen; frazzled woman
in a torn red sweater, picking Sundays off the floor,
a speckle drifting in the dust of thumped cushions.
She could leave. Slip off into bright air, between
birch and viney arch, swing to and fro, blankly. But,
in the hearth, the nest of still warm ashes, neat ghosts.

BLUES

This room smacks
of a familiar mood. Stale
curtains droop; the corners
dim in a conspiracy
of winter accomplices –
those brash magazines thrown
among the poetry and hardbacks;
the promises, promises of
holiday brochures sink
into a wreckage of bumf.

The wardrobe wallows
in its own mid-
life crisis. Nothing fits
on coathangers or in drawers.
The heavy door gapes
on the sad bulge of misfit,
impulse buys and, worn once,
a ball-gown slumped
in a purple-dark sulk.

Outdoors, the heaped sky holds
no hope. Beneath the smog
the world is grey
on grey. Yet, it must
be Spring – there, by the path,
a crocus thrusts, and something
pernickety
as instinct shifts and warns
it is time to straighten up.

To untack the cobwebs,
push the windows wide.
Let in the music that floats
from the tangle of the beech,
where, in the queer light,
a blackbird lords it in full throat.

WEEDS

After I had slashed the briars
snarled around the lilac bush, levelled
nettles, ganging up, idle as thugs
in a corner, I dug the fork deep
under thistle's rooted thickenings,
then, with brute force, stunted
ruddy docks flourishing between the rocks

I could not move. I crawled,
hands streaked with pain, to claw
down among the torsions of the scutch
where the blade of the hoe
would free nothing. After I had unwed
dandelions, all hugger-mugger,
from their for-ever-after beds,

I straightened slowly up
to stretch my back, and
to ask myself why it is,
that delicate human beings
are known as weeds.

THORN

How can I grasp this dream; this bine
that seeds from ditch to ditch, greens
hedgerows, riots colour down the glens,
shapes blood-ripe berries for a world
beyond this body, so exquisitely contrived
for pain, snapped from the probe
and force of sterile steel I wake to.

Always, blooming, I am there ahead
of quick cold hands that pry
into the secret chapters of the flesh,
words, dropped like stones to rattle
down the brain's incline. Leaping,
on the giddy slopes, I thrust
into the bright, unbroken blue.

The breeze is a song of fragrance;
flower jewels, small miracles of life,
blaze up, tantalise me. There I lose
ground, turn to find the way back
obstructed with monstrous growths.
Now in darkness, every hill's an ogre
set to pounce. On tangled briars

I bleed flesh, and now my footing's
gone, slow fall until at a scream's sound
this body lies still where pain winces
off dim walls. The mind again begins
its hypodermic calm. Am I wrong
to want a dream, vigorous and wild,
grafted to the moment of awakening.

FOR THIS DAY

Today her soft room gleams behind
windows pushed wide
on to a sky that is stretched
to the limit of its blue;
along the hedge bob sun-struck daffodils
excited by each other's gold.
She hugs this joy warily – a fragile thing,
or unmeant gift, which might be snatched away.

Downstairs, routine kitchen sounds
are roots of the ordinary day
and, in pubescent chaos,
her children shave the springy grass
to within an inch of its newfound life.
From high delicate branches a blackbird
splits the ether with its song.
The air is linen-fresh.

All round her this brute life thrusts:
its hormones, heartbeats, the swell
of tender buds dares her
to forget the unriddable: the quick
cold hands, cold words
dropped in those textbook rooms; clever
death's hungry probe
down the blood to where she is now,
contained in an unsweet discipline...

Know each blossoming to be the emblem
of survival and the reprieve
alive in that doctor's candid eyes
and for this day
unclinch.
Let go this pain.
Blink at its wet-winged giddy flight.

A Young Woman with a Child
  ## on Each Hand

A young woman with a child on each hand
turns at the zebra crossing
to join two more young women,
one pregnant, one tilting a pram.
She is vital, almost beautiful.
Her sons are sturdy and neat.
She walks into the life I am leaving.

When she greets her friends, I am aware
mothercraft has blinded her, till anxiety
thins her voice. I want to call out,
that for her, now is filled

with simple certainties – a spilled cup,
a rowdy room, a bed-time story. But
as she moves down the street, I can
only guess the weight
of her sacrifice, her tenderness
as her hands keep emptying, emptying...

LETTING GO

The false security
of the simple
and the ordinary.

I lift the latch, push,
take several steps
across the bright linoleum
toward the dresser shouting,
'Kids, kids, I can hardly hear my ears,'
when I realise I am in a dream.

The fool in me
not wanting to accept change.

In that moment I had my children
as I still want them to be. Kilts
and knee-socks, short pants
and t-shirts. The soft splash
as milk
falls from the tray of the high chair.
I'm reaching back to them
from chat through chores
to play. What I didn't know then . . .
That rowdy kitchen was a piece
of cake. I ruled the roost.

Now these young men and women
sprawl over so much space
they scare me. The world's
the oyster their minds
prise wide. They talk

inches above my head. Their
laughter and their language leap
beyond me.   Now

I am forced to look at time
in another way. Not
as so many grains of sand
flowing from glass belly
to glass belly, but how,
through the persistent gnawing
of years, I've weathered
as I watch them grow. And
how at last, as I let go
and slip behind them, I ease
my bones into the universe.

III

ANCIENT GARDEN

To this ancient garden I am
a future ghost. A pale shape
in its tiredness that waters and weeds.
A warm pressure on the wintry earth,
a kneeling form bedding in plants
hopefully, like a pilgrim at a shrine.

It is aware of me, in its own scheme,
and tolerates the changes caused by my
succession. Feels, itself, wearied
by the seasonal round – the prunings,
the mulchings. A spate of wilderness
tangling its fragrances and it will know
that I have passed on.

It will be lost, of course, but slowly,
and not in my time. A beech tree
or a haze of blue-bells survives
for generations. But my devotion
will fall from it, evaporate. My
excesses and mistakes will run
riot to clog its furthest edges.

Though the clipped yew trees
those Victorian enthusiasts shaped
stand vigorous and green at any time,
a frail woman, her life grown thin,
would petrify if she did not move.
Would whiten among their harled roots.

STONE DOORSTEP

You were all we salvaged
from the demolition; grey
slab of stone. Your topside

rubbed to a hard shine by
countless feet. They strained,
Pat and Jem, to shift you

from your old bed
at the kitchen door.
And on your rough rump

we saw carved, 'cut
and hefted by P. and J.
1784'.

Now you serve in the archway
on our new patio, where
lavender and pale green leaves

bush. Still
it's all the same to you
who walks on you, or

in what time. We
take no such chance.
Before you were re-set

you were branded,
'hauled by P. and J.
1984'.

WRITTEN BECAUSE OF SARAH W. DAVIES, 1882

I want her Victorian life-style,
her regular, solid thinking:
to make the mornings brisk,

from letters written and ordered meals,
to afternoons of croquet
with tea on the lawn, or directing,

in threadwork and folds, the linen guild,
on to sedate suppers mellowing to evenings
of quiet talk, a little music and books.

I have her house –
her black silk, ivory-handled umbrella
to step primly out to church.

I have her polished mahogany knee-desk,
its ornate, tagged key, its secret drawer.
I have her book of transcribed poems

and psalms in her delicate, deliberate hand,
its pressed flowers and traceries of grass
a bonus of calm between creamy gilt-edged pages.

She lives all round me:
in the faint jangle of bells below stairs,
in faded lavender sachets in cupboards –

When, at bedtime, round my doorway,
her restive, long skirts bring their whisperings,
I would stop my heart, let her enter into me.

FORCES

Unleashed, hostile, the wind came.
Its bayings had this house
like a signboard, creaking and slamming,
all night out on the hill. It whipped

chimney-pots like spinning-tops,
and tackled slates like a team of
arm-wrestlers in enforced residence.
The wind pushed windowpanes trembling

into bedrooms, letting the sleet
flush us from our dreamy blue
to a gun-grey habitation. Powerless,
we watched the wind maul the beech tree

and lash out at the silver birch. Where
ivy clutched grey ash bark, the wind
paused; whetted lacquered claws to savage
the trellis and bleed rosebuds. It reared

to gnaw the yew tree then, spat it out
bottle green. The wind harried
and snapped at the washline till
the flustered reds, yellows and blues

flopped like rag dolls in the wet. Far up,
rooks, gulls were its crazed trapeze act.
We could not stand near the wind.
It beat our heads and shoved us back.

Our eyeballs stung from its fierce slap.
We feared this wind had come to get us.
It seemed nothing, man-made or mortal,
was safe in its manic attack. Except,

lodged in our glasshouse, all flesh,
the freshly decked Nelly Moser stood
untouched, in all her wide-eyed pink,
and observed this crude performance.

                                        Remote, calm.
A pale, thin delicate lady.

LAPSE

On Sunday, I found a bowl of
over-ripe plums, juiced and fermenting,
on a too-warm, forgotten shelf, and
from the heaped flesh came the smell

of picked fruit left to moulder
in a dim corner of a childhood
years away in another county,
a half-remembered room where the light

slowed purple as the underside
of a berried bush, and that
yeasting sweetness climbed my nostrils
and coloured the whole house.

And I gorged on the pungent memory
all day long till our street lay
bone white beneath the sodium glare,
and the late October night thinned with ice.

SHE WINDS THE CLOCK

for Susan Connolly

All year the dated calendar
hung above the empty shelves;
naked and brown-boned, winter
stretched there, a lone robin
on guard.

      March gusted, turned
paths to lakes. Its April was
rain and shine, rain and shine
on bruised pink. Of the deep scars
black-edged May had shaped
only the house in its stopped
heart could tell.

      Summer slipped by, bursts
of colour and fragrance ignored.
The cock pheasant, brilliant
among flaring stalks, lifted autumn
into another season...

      Advent, and the young woman,
like a new broom, came.   A clock
ticked: dust flew, firelight danced
with shadow; pots muttered. The months,
updated, beckoned.

They heave with goodness now, the shelves –
dark puddings brim in chalk bowls,
citrus rind ambers in glossy jars,
chutney traps tangs and spices; cheese,
the soft curds clotting gauze, and,
against the wall, white and blue china.
Then oranges, golden like captive moons. .

Christmas, applewood sparks, the air
is pollened beneath the scent; pale,
she breaks new-risen bread.
Around her, objects, reassured,
settle like friends. Under her heart
a chrysalis of hope moves
on the breath of butterfly wings.

She winds the clock.

NEWGRANGE

Then they came among the boulders
                              sleeping
in the loop of the river
and roused them into
a toiling mass and made a house
of stone. A tomb
to replace the womb.

Where they padded down to douse
their jaded bodies in the swell,
or tended their beasts from place
to place, they made paths.

A slab-stone hoisted to a lintel
their heads bowed under often
to gently fold their dead.   And
on the stones inside the passage grave
they carved their art. Runes
to mock the puckered brow of science.

What if they offered blood.
                              Appeased,
each late December's dawn, their god,
the Sun bathes
that stilly chamber to reveal how,
with cup-marks, spirals and a single fern
they praised in their intent, knowing
that all living is a death.

THE SEAL OFF CLOGHERHEAD
for Mim and Ruth - October 1987

Turns, flips, bobs, is still; teasing
he slides, dives, disappears and
is back riving the surfboard waves.

He is another fantasy
out among the phantom ships.
He tells his secrets to no one.

We drift here, on yellow sand, in heady
autumn heat to watch the Mournes'
blue dip and peak and thrill

to see him again in this same place:
oil-sleek, lamp-eyed acrobat,
thick dark vein to the sea's flow.

SITTING ON A ROCK IN LETTERFRACK
for Hugo

Alone on the rock
beside the fuchsia bush,
surrounded by stones
and mossy things. The sky
blue with cotton cloud. The sea
breathes and breathes

out in the bay – a soft sound
as easily overlooked
as my own breath. In the fuchsia,
the motor of a thousand bees
drones steady
and comforting. On this rock

I fear nothing. I am
a part of the lichen
and the stones. I breathe
in private with the sea. Stray,
thinned fragments of my soul
unite, and housed, find calm.

A bee flies toward me
in the light, out of the fuchsia's
dark globe. He dips,
homing, circling me,
circling me. He has journeyed
around the whole planet. He has
flown across the centuries
from the hives of an old, old

world. He gives back to me
the skinny little girl,
with sun-striped hair,
running in the wind. He
returns my mother
in her yellow dress,
and the squashed plum
inside my schoolbag.

DOGROSES

In winter, the briars lash
like cat-o'-nine-tails, their
unleashed power a scourge
to Sunday sweaters or un-
suspecting flesh. Take
that, and that, and that
they snarl, wild in their attack.

Under the whip of the weather
they too must know their point
of stress. And though they scratch
and fight amongst themselves,
their pinks
are beautiful, in summer,
slavering the hedgerows.

A Middling Day

Under unbearable blue, today,
the beach lay tucked white
with emptied shells. The sea
inhaled, exhaled, wearied
by so many deaths. In the pale
shallows, the children squealed and ran
tearing up the salt lace. Overhead,
low convoys of shorebirds flew
above the caravans to where fields
stirred, husk-green, deep as water;
and the birdscare gave out dull thuds
all day, like distant bombs.

Now the tide is on the turn, and
people have crunched back
to the swollen dunes, drifting
up the sandy slopes to the flicker
and pulse of summer homes, to shape
the hot night into those dreams
the flesh topples. Into a sky
plunged in mystery the white moon rides;
the one sleepless eye, watchful,
after this middling day, of the sea's
drag on its silver rein, this silted
head, this blood thinning.

TREE-PLANTING

I

Young trees left out in darkness,
an abandoned wheelbarrow, black plastic
merging with the night.
Weathered tools rest in the dark shed.

The tired woman comes in, eats
and goes to bed.
A forty watt moon lights the windy slopes.

II

Muddy boots stiffen by the doorjamb.
The clock stares from the wall.

She sleeps. She dreams
her body is younger, her bones strong.
A storm blows up. The moon hides.
She is struggling to stand in the wind.
Tamped in clay, her feet are immobile.
Her skin is becoming ridged and hard.

But her blood is woman,
it will not give in.
Her body fights and sways, heaving.
She wakes, trembling and cold.
She has won.

III

It is morning. Another tree planting day.
She drags on the clumsy boots.
Goes out to where the earth
waits to receive each sapling,
the tender, straw-balled roots.

LAWRENCE FAGAN

deaf-mute artist, born Drogheda, c. 1820 - 1895

These ruins are clenched. Their grey stones
will not reward you. Blackthorn and nettle
guard the gaps of each crumbling form -
arch, gable and scriptured cross. You
love them, know them inside out: caress

their cloistered shapeliness, slow prospect
their bare defensiveness – those flanks
and cleavages of exposed time. Mute,
you exist in their unchanging cry.
In sullen, wind-stropped days your quick pen

sketches their multiple scars as you crouch
in the lee of a tombstone, or in summer,
sprawl in a hot smudge of buttercups. How
sound and remote they stand, their
high towers named through the mists

of meaning, while you struggle in silence
in these narrow streets of Drogheda,
sidling in to the Whitehorse Hotel
to exchange your art for ale –
that harsh eroding of your hopes and dreams.

Your melancholy sits heavy in you,
moistens the deep stress of your eyes;
soaks up the single patronage
that could make a monument of your name,
then unsteadies and stops your hand.

Soon death must trundle your talent
into an unmarked grave, so that nobody hears
your exact, clean voice of stone, or traces
the infinite freedom in your skill,
shares your walled-in-pain.

A Backwards Look

It is strange the way I used to think
my centuries-old and hip-thatched kitchen,
deep in the back of the house,
shut me in from the world,
hived me into its poverty –
how each small window doled out the light
in grimed swatches. A puzzle
of sky and rooftops I jigsawed
from sink to dresser to stove.

Strange, because now in this brand-new,
green and oak-trimmed room, bathed
in the shine of picture windows,
where I desert
my brood, the pots, this day
to lean on the bright glass and gaze;
the hardness and chill against my skin
carries me into an abandoned place,
a state of mind in which I clearly see...

Light reflected from the stable wall
knife into the cobbled alley;
where sad women-shapes,
hung with sharp-faced children,
peer from the smoke-filled cottages;
where sullen men stumble out to spit
and piss at the moon, where strays
prowl and watch
to scavenge the thickening stench.